T's Big Book of Cuss

Word Alternatives

1,001 Words and Phrases You Can Use

Instead of Swearing

T. Cathers-Mitchell

This book is dedicated to all you motherfathers! Seriously!

This book is dedicated to all you parents, grandparents,

aunts, uncles, teachers and anyone else who comes into

contact with children and need to learn to control their

potty mouths. I hope you enjoy this book as much as I did

putting it together!

T. Cathers-Mitchell

Preface

Several years ago, I had an idea! People were always giggling and complimenting me on the words and phrases I used instead of swearing. I have two children, and always felt the need to control my language around them.

One day, I was online, searching for new words and phrases to use, reading many of them aloud to my sister. We were having a blast reading what other parents and grandparents had come up with. Therefore, I decided to compile and publish an article on HubPages, entitled "101 Great Cuss/Swear Word Alternatives." It was an instant hit! As soon as I posted a link on Facebook, it was shared all over the country within a few days!

Seeing the success of the first article, and because I had so much fun putting it together, I decided to compile and publish a second list of 101 words and phrases, entitled, "Holy Rackafratz! 101 More Funny Swear/Cuss

Word Alternatives. Together, the two articles have had over 250,000 views since 2011.

After five years, these two articles on HubPages are still going strong. So, I thought, "Why not turn them into a book?" So I combined my two 101 lists, and decided to turn 202 into 1,001! I consulted my friends, family, other parents and grandparents, aunts, uncles, cousins from the World Wide Web to compile this masterpiece. So, here it is! 1,001 mothersmucking cuss word alternatives! Enjoy!

Acknowledgements

I would like to thank the many people who helped this book come into being. A big thank you to my friends and family, for sharing their own cuss word alternatives and those of their friends and family. I would also like to thank my children for helping me come up with some new ones based on the movies and television shows that they watch. And last, but not least, I would like to thank the parents, grandparents, aunts, uncles and cousins from across the wonderful World Wide Web for sharing their words and phrases online. You all have been an integral part of this compilation. You all rule!

T. Cathers-Mitchell

T's Big Book of Cuss Word Alternatives:

1001 Words and Phrases You Can Use Instead of Swearing

1. A Curse on Both Your Houses!

2. Abominations!

3. Absurd!

4. Aflac!

5. A-Hole!

6. Ain't That a Witch?

7. Amazeballs!

8. Anus!

9. Apostrophe!

10. Applesauce!

11. Arrgh!

12. Arugula!

13. Aunt Annie's Alligator!

14. Avada Kedavra!

15. Aw, Baby Ducks!

16. Aw, Duck Water!

17. Aw, Man!

18. Aw, Noodles!

19. Ay Ay Ay!

20. Ay Carumba!

21. Ay Chihuahua!

22. B.S.

23. Bad Word, Bad Word, Bad Word!

24. Bah, Humbug!

25. Balderdash!

26. Balls!

27. Baloney Sausage!

28. Banana Sandwiches!

29. Banana Shenanigans!

30. Bangkok!

31. Baps!

32. Barbara Streisand!

33. Barber, Baby, Bubbles and a Bumble Bee!

34. Barnacles!

35. Bastages!

36. Bazinga!

37. Beans and Rice!

38. Beans and Weenies!

39. Bed Presser!

40. Begone!

41. Bejabbers!

42. Bejeebus!

43. Beknighted Toadspawn!

44. Belgium!

45. Billions of Bilious Blue Blistering Barnacles!

46. Blangdang!

47. Blankhole!

48. Blasphemer!

49. Blasphemy!

50. Blast it!

51. Blast!

52. Bleep the Bleep Up!

53. Bleep!

54. Bless Your Heart!

55. Blessed Fig's End!

56. Blimey!

57. Blistering Barnacles!

58. Blockhead!

59. Blood and Bloody Ashes!

60. Blood and Sand!

61. Bloody!

62. Blurgh!

63. Bob Saget!

64. Bocce Balls!

65. Bogus!

66. Boiling Butterbeer!

67. Bollocks!

68. Bologna Sandwich!

69. Bolsheviks!

70. Bonehead!

71. Boo!

72. Boogersnot!

73. Booty!

74. Bosh!

75. Botheration!

76. Botox!

77. Bottom!

78. Botulism!

79. Bozos!

80. Brandywine!

81. Brother!

82. Bug Off!

83. Bugger

84. Bugger My Toe!

85. Buggeration!

86. Bull Chips!

87. Bull Dinkie!

88. Bull Feathers!

89. Bull Hickey!

90. Bull Poo!

91. Bull Shirt!

92. Bull Spit!

93. Bull Twinkies!

94. Bullfrogs in Heat!

95. Bullsnot!

96. Bum Looker!

97. Bum!

98. Bumfiddler!

99. Bummer!

100.   Bun of a Sitch!

101.   Butter Beans!

102.   Butterball!

103.   Butterfinger!

104.   Butterscotch!

105.   Butthead!

106.   Buttocks!

107.   Buttonhole!

108.   Butts!

109.   By God's Nails!

110.   By Jingo!

111.   By Jovi!

112.   By My Hairy Legs!

113.   By Saint Boogar and All the Saints at the

    Backside Door of Purgatory!

114.   By the Beard of Zeus!

115.   By the Double-Barreled Jumping Jimnetty!

116.   By the Power of Greyskull!

117.   Caca Face!

118.   Caca Head!

119.   Caca!

120.   Caesar's ghost!

121.   Calamity Jane!

122. Calvary!

123. Camel on the Ceiling!

124. Captain Kirk's Nipples!

125. Casserole!

126. Castigation!

127. Catsandratsandelephants!

128. Chalice!

129. Charlatans!

130. Charles Dickens!

131. Cheeky Monkey!

132. Cheese and Crackers!

133. Cheese and Rice!

134. Cheese Whiz!

135. Cheeseburgers!

136. Cheeses!

137. Chicken Noodle Soup!

138. Chit!

139. Chizz!

140.   Christ on a Bike!

141.   Christ on a Cracker!

142.   Christmas on a Cracker!

143.   Chronicles of Narnia!

144.   Cinnamon Sticks!

145.   Clinkers!

146.   Cloff-Prunker!

147.   Clown Shoes!

148.   Coconuts!

149.   Cods!

150.   Condemnation!

151.   Confound and Confiscate!

152.   Confound It!

153.   Confuddle and Befound!

154.   Consarn!

155.   Cornnuts!

156.   Cotton-Headed Ninny Muggins!

157.   Cottonpickin!

158.   Cougar's Call!

159.   Cowabunga!

160.   Crab Nuggets!

161.   Cracker Jacks!

162.   Crackydack!

163.   Crap on a Cracker!

164.   Crap!

165.   Crapola!

166.   Crappity!

167.   Crappy-Doodles!

168.   Crayola!

169.   Crikey!

170.   Criminalities!

171.   Criminy!

172.   Crucio!

173.   Crud Munchkins!

174.   Crud!

175.   Crudbucket!

176.   Crudmuffin!

177.   Crumbs!

178.   Crummidy Dum Dum!

179.   Crunch Poop!

180.   Curse Word!

181.   Curses of Curses!

182.   Curses!

183.   D'OH!

184.   Dad Blast It!

185.   Dad Burnit!

186.   Dadgummit!

187.   Dad-Sizzle!

188.   Dagbling!

189.   Dagnabbit!

190.   Damn it All to High Heaven!

191.   Damn it All to Kingdom Come!

192.   Damnation!

193.   Dang Rabbit!

194. Dang!

195. Dargondabble!

196. Darjeeling!

197. Darn Tootin'!

198. Darn!

199. Darnation

200. Day-um!

201. D-Bag!

202. Derp!

203. Derriere!

204. Diddley!

205. Diddly Squat!

206. Didgeridoo!

207. Dill-Headed Winker Toss!

208. Dillweed!

209. Dingbat!

210. Dingleberry!

211. Dinglehopper!

212.   Dingo's Kidneys!

213.   Dink!

214.   Dip-a-dee-do-da!

215.   Dipstick!

216.   Dirt Nap!

217.   Dirty Rackafratz!

218.   Dirty Word!

219.   Dishonor! Dishonor on You. Dishonor on

Your Cow…!

220.   Dobby's Sock!

221.   Dod Gammit!

222.   Dog Biscuit!

223.   Donald Trump Hair!

224.   Donald Trump!

225.   Donkey!

226.   Donkey!

227.   Donut Holes!

228.   Doo Doo!

229.   Doodle!

230.   Doodlebugs!

231.   Doofus!

232.   Dookie Salad!

233.   Dookie!

234.   Dope!

235.   Dragon Ball Z!

236.   Dragonflies!

237.   Drat It!

238.   Drat!

239.   Dream a Dozen Donuts!

240.   Dude!

241.   Dumb Head!

242.   Dummy!

243.   Dung!

244.   Ear, Egg Elephant!

245.   Eat It!

246.   Eat my Chocolate Swirl Shake!

247.   Eat My Shorts!

248.   Eat Slugs!

249.   Eat Soap!

250.   Eek the Cat!

251.   Eek!

252.   Eep!

253.   Effervescence!

254.   Egad!

255.   Eureka!

256.   Excellent!

257.   Exclamation Points!

258.   Expelliarmus!

259.   Expletive Deleted!

260.   Expletive!

261.   F!

262.   Fack!

263.   Fahrvergnugen!

264.   Fairy Godmother!

265. Fala Fudge Keys!

266. Fanny!

267. Fardle!

268. Farg!

269. Fargin' Icehole!

270. Farkcicles!

271. Fart Knocker!

272. Feck off!

273. Feldercarb!

274. Female Dog!

275. Fiddle Faddle!

276. Fiddle-Dee-Dee!

277. Fiddlesniddle!

278. Fiddlesticks!

279. Fie On It!

280. Fig Newtons!

281. Figwit!

282. Filthy Word!

283.   Firecrackers!

284.   Fish 'N Chips!

285.   Fish Nuggets!

286.   Fish Paste!

287.   Fish Sniffer!

288.   Fishsticks!

289.   Flabbergast!

290.   Flack!

291.   Flame's Alive!

292.   Flaming Heck!

293.   Flank!

294.   Flapdoodle!

295.   Flarn!

296.   Flibbertigibbit!

297.   Flick!

298.   Flimflammery!

299.   Flipping Flapjacks!

300.   Flipping Frogs!

301.   Flocking!

302.   Fluck You!

303.   Fluck!

304.   Fluff Muffin!

305.   Fluffernuts!

306.   FML!

307.   Fock Dock!

308.   Fookin'!

309.   Fool!

310.   For Crying Out Loud!

311.   For Fake's Sake!

312.   For Heaven's Sake!

313.   For Pete's sake!

314.   For Pity's Sake!

315.   For the Love of Everything!

316.   For the Love of Mike!

317.   For the Love of Pete!

318.   Ford Crown Victoria in a Sweater at

Christmas!

319.   Ford it All!

320.   Fork!

321.   Forkin'

322.   Fother Mucker!

323.   Four Duck Steaks!

324.   Four Fluffy Feathers on a Fiffer Feffer Feff!

325.   Four-Letter Word!

326.   Frack!

327.   Fracking!

328.   Fragdaggle!

329.   Fraggle Rock!

330.   Frazzle Fart!

331.   Freaking!

332.   Frick Frack!

333.   Frick on a Stick!

334.   Frick!

335.   Frickity!

336.   Fried Green Tomatoes!

337.   Friggin!

338.   Friggin' A!

339.   Fruits!

340.   Fuddy Duddy!

341.   Fuddyduds!

342.   Fudge Berries!

343.   Fudge Buckets!

344.   Fudge Cake!

345.   Fudge Nuggets!

346.   Fudge Off!

347.   Fudge Sauce!

348.   Fudge the Bucket!

349.   Fudge!

350.   Fudgecicles

351.   Fudgesicles on a Corn Stick!

352.   Fudgey-Fudgers!

353. Fudrucker!

354. Fug!

355. Full of Horse Apples!

356. Full of Soup!

357. Fumadiddle!

358. Funk You!

359. Funk!

360. Funky Nuggets!

361. Fut the Wuck?

362. G. Rover Cripes!

363. Gadzooks!

364. Galloping Gremlins!

365. Garfunkel!

366. Gargoyle Nose!

367. Gawd!

368. Gee Whiz!

369. Gee Willickers!

370. Gee!

371.   Geez Louise!

372.   Geez Terwilligers!

373.   Geez!

374.   Get Bent!

375.   Get Lost!

376.   Get Out of Town!

377.   Giant Gumdrops!

378.   Giggity!

379.   Gilbert Godfrey!

380.   Give Me a Break!

381.   Glaring Jellyfish!

382.   Glory Be!

383.   Glory!

384.   Go Blow it Out Your Ear!

385.   Go Elf Yourself!

386.   Go Fly a Kite!

387.   Go Fork Yourself!

388.   Go Jump in a Lake!

389.   Go Lick a Duck!

390.   Go Smurf Yourself!

391.   Go Stuff Yourself!

392.   Go to Halifax!

393.   Goat, Girl, Goo-goo Goggles!

394.   Gobbledygook!

395.   Gobshites!

396.   God Bless America!

397.   God Bless It!

398.   Godblankit!

399.   Goddawg!

400.   Golly Gee!

401.   Golly Neds!

402.   Good Gravy!

403.   Good Heavens!

404.   Good Night Nurse!

405.   Good Night!

406.   Goodness Gracious!

407.   Goof Nugget!

408.   Gorram!

409.   Gorrammit!

410.   Gorsh!

411.   Gosh Dang It!

412.   Gosh Darn it!

413.   Gosh Darn!

414.   Gosh!

415.   Gosh-All-Potomac!

416.   Gracious Me!

417.   Gramercy!

418.   Grasshole!

419.   Gravity Works!

420.   Great Balls of Fire!

421.   Great Galaxies!

422.   Great Galloping Guppies!

423.   Great God in the Foothills!

424.   Great Googly Moogly!

425.   Great Green Gobs of Gopher Guts!

426.   Great Horn Spoon!

427.   Great Odin's Raven!

428.   Great Scott!

429.   Grizzle!

430.   Grrr!

431.   GTFO!

432.   Gul Dumit!

433.   Hades!

434.   Hagrid's Buttcrack!

435.   Hairy Hobbit Feet!

436.   Halfling Hoards!

437.   Halfwit!

438.   Hallelujah!

439.   Hamburgers!

440.   Hanna Banera!

441.   Hardboiled Hotdogs!

442.   Haystacks!

443. Heavens Above!

444. Heavens to Betsy!

445. Heavens to Murgatroid!

446. Heck and Double Heck!

447. Heck!

448. Heckfire!

449. H-E-Double-Hockey-Sticks!

450. Hellen Keller with a Bad Haircut!

451. Hello, Nurse!

452. Hen in a Hat!

453. Heretics!

454. Hi-Diddly-Ho!

455. Hind Side!

456. Hiney!

457. Hippopotomus!

458. Hocus Pokus!

459. Hogswallop!

460. Hogwash!

461.   Holy Bejeebus!

462.   Holy Bird Turd!

463.   Holy Bologna!

464.   Holy Buckets!

465.   Holy Carp!

466.   Holy Cheeses!

467.   Holy Cheezits!

468.   Holy Chimp!

469.   Holy Cow!

470.   Holy Crap!

471.   Holy Cripes on Toast

472.   Holy Crumpets!

473.   Holy Frijoles!

474.   Holy Fudge Nuts!

475.   Holy Gaboly!

476.   Holy Giblets!

477.   Holy Goodness!

478.   Holy Guacamole!

479.   Holy Hand Grenade of Antioch!

480.   Holy Heck Specks!

481.   Holy Humus!

482.   Holy Jalapeno!

483.   Holy Jumped-Up Blue Mud!

484.   Holy Kachow!

485.   Holy Macaroni!

486.   Holy Moley Macaroni!

487.   Holy Moly!

488.   Holy Mother!

489.   Holy Rusted Metal, Batman!

490.   Holy Schistosoma!

491.   Holy Schizophrenia!

492.   Holy Schlitz!

493.   Holy Shibblets!

494.   Holy Shnikies!

495.   Holy Smokes!

496.   Holy Snapping Turtles!

497.   Holy World of Goo!

498.   Holy Wow!

499.   Hoover Dam!

500.   Horrors!

501.   Horse Feathers!

502.   Horse Hockey!

503.   Horse Patooie!

504.   Horse Pucky!

505.   Hot Diggity!

506.   Hot Peppers!

507.   Howdy Doody!

508.   Humbug!

509.   I Don't Give a Donald Duck!

510.   I Swear to Christmas!

511.   I'll be Gobsmacked!

512.   I've had it!

513.   Ice Cream!

514.   Ichabod is Itchy!

515.   Idiot!

516.   Idjits!

517.   Imbecile!

518.   Imperio!

519.   Inconceivable!

520.   Infidels!

521.   Jabberwockies!

522.   Jabberwocky!

523.   Jackrabbitdonkey!

524.   Jagweed!

525.   Jean-Claude VanDamme!

526.   Jeebus Cripes!

527.   Jeebus!

528.   Jeepers Creepers!

529.   Jeepers!

530.   Jeesum Crow!

531.   Jeezy Creezy!

532.   Jerk Water!

533.   Jerry Jordan's Jelly Jar!

534.   Jesus Wept!

535.   Jesus, Mary and Joseph!

536.   Jiminy Crickets!

537.   Jiminy Hee Ha!

538.   Jinkies!

539.   Judas Priest!

540.   Julius Caesar!

541.   Jumped Up Jeebies!

542.   Jumpin' Catfish!

543.   Jumpin' Jehoshaphat!

544.   Jumpin' Jesus on a Pogostick!

545.   Jumpin' Jiminy!

546.   Justin Bieber!

547.   Keyboard!

548.   Kiester!

549.   Kiss my Buns!

550.   Kiss My Grits!

551.   Kiss my Madagascar Fanny Pack!

552.   Kite Strings!

553.   Kitty Whiskers!

554.   Knickers!

555.   Knucklehead!

556.   Kuku Bananas!

557.   Kumquat!

558.   La La Lou!

559.   Lady Toots!

560.   Lazy Lion Licks a Lollipop!

561.   Leapin' Lizards!

562.   Leonardo Da Vinci!

563.   Lickety Split!

564.   Lightning Bugs!

565.   Like Fun You Are!

566.   Lily-Livered Milk Drinker!

567.   Lint Licker!

568.   Lions and Tigers and Bears. Oh, My!

569.   Lord, Love a Duck!

570.   Lordy!

571.   Love a Duck!

572.   Lump Off!

573.   M'Kay!

574.   Malarkey!

575.   Malediction!

576.   Malkovich!

577.   Mallius Maleficarum!

578.   Mamma Mia!

579.   Margaret Thatcher naked on a Cold Day!

580.   Marklar!

581.   Marmalade!

582.   Me Oh My!

583.   Meanie Head!

584.   Meanie Weenie!

585.   Mecrob!

586.   Mercedes Benz!

587.   Merlin's Beard!

588.   Merlin's Pants!

589.   Merlin's Pink Tutu!

590.   Merlin's Toe Socks!

591.   Middle Finger!

592.   Milk and Cookies!

593.   Monkey Flunker!

594.   Monkey Poo!

595.   Moonrocks!

596.   Motha Jumpa!

597.   Mother Bear!

598.   Mother Blanker!

599.   Mother Father!

600.   Mother Flaming Poodles!

601.   Mother Fletcher!

602.   Mother Flunker!

603.   Mother Francis!

604.   Mother Hubbard!

605.   Mother Lover!

606.   Mother Moth!

607.   Mother of Butter!

608.   Mother of Goodness!

609.   Mother of Pearl!

610.   Mother Puffin!

611.   Mother Pus Bucket!

612.   Mother Scratcher!

613.   Mother…fatherbrothersister!

614.   Motherpucker!

615.   Mothersmucker!

616.   Mousepad!

617.   Muffliato!

618.   Muppet!

619.   Mustang Sally!

620.   My Arse!

621.   My Giddy Aunt!

622.   My Word!

623.   Mylanta!

624.   Narf!

625.   Naughty Word!

626.   Nerd Head!

627.   Nerfherder!

628.   Nertz!

629.   Nimrod!

630.   No-No!

631.   Nonsense!

632.   Noodle Crutch!

633.   Notafinga!

634.   Nuckin Futs!

635.   Numbnuts!

636.   Numbskull!

637.   Nut Bunnies!

638.   O. M. Freakin` G!

639.   Obscenity!

640.   Oh Bother and Blow It!

641.   Oh Boy!

642.   Oh Darn!

643.   Oh My Damn!

644.   Oh My Dog!

645.   Oh My Glob!

646.   Oh My Goodness!

647.   Oh My Gosh!

648.   Oh My Heck!

649.   Oh My Land!

650.   Oh My Peas!

651.   Oh My Sainted Trousers!

652.   Oh My Stars and Garters!

653.   Oh My Stars!

654.   Oh My!

655.   Oh Truck!

656.   Oh Woe!

657.   Oh, Balls!

658.   Oh, Bark!

659.   Oh, Bother!

660.   Oh, Buggers!

661.   Oh, Carm Cakes!

662.   Oh, Crumbs!

663.   Oh, Dear!

664.   Oh, Firetruck!

665.   Oh, Fish Hooks!

666.   Oh, For Crying in the Night!

667.   Oh, Knickers!

668.   Oh, Man!

669.   Oh, Nipples!

670.   Oh, Sheep!

671.   Oh, Ship!

672.   Oh, Shoot the Cat!

673.   Oh, Smeg!

674.   Oh, Snap!

675.   Okey Dokey Smokey!

676.   Okily Dokily!

677.   OMG!

678.   Ouch!

679.   Paltry Poultice of Pigeon!

680.   Pantalones!

681.   Panther's Paw!

682.   Pants!

683.   Pat Sajak

684.   Peanut butter and jelly!

685.   Peapods!

686.   Peas and Rice!

687.   Perdition!

688.   Petrificus Totalus!

689.   Phooey!

690.   Phosphorous!

691.   Pickled Pansy!

692.   Pickles!

693.   Piddle!

694.   Piece of Carp!

695.   Piece of Jerk!

696.   Piece of Trash!

697.   Piffle!

698.   Pigs in a Blanket!

699.   Pimento Loaf!

700.   Pintos and Cheese!

701.   Pish!

702.   Pisser!

703.   Pixie Sticks!

704.   Ploopy!

705.   Pluck a Duck!

706.   Pluck It!

707.   Plum Diddly!

708.   Pokémon!

709.   Poo Head!

710.   Poo on a Stick!

711.   Poo!

712.   Poop Knuckle!

713.   Poop!

714.   Poopie-head!

715.   Poopyscoop!

716.   Poppycock!

717.   Posterior!

718.   Pouty Pinatas!

719.   Powdered Sugar Brownies!

720.   Profanity!

721.   Pumpernickel!

722.   Quacking Quackeroo!

723.   Quick Queen of Quincy!

724.   Quotation Marks!

725.   Ramen!

726.   Ramma-Lamma-Ding-Dong!

727.   Raspberries!

728.   Rasputin!

729.   Rassin-Frassin!

730.   Rat Turds!

731.   Rat-bag!

732.   Rats!

733.   Razzafraggin!

734.   Razzleberry Dressing!

735.   Rear End!

736.   Rectory!

737.   Rhubarb!

738.   Right in the Poodle's noodle!

739.   Rubbish!

740.   Rucka Frucka!

741.   Sacrilege!

742.   Saints Preserve Us!

743.   Sam Hill!

744.   Sayonara!

745.   Schmoogies!

746.   Scrunt-Faced Scroll!

747.   Scuddlebutt!

748.   Sectumsempra!

749.   Shamalama!

750.   Shards!

751.   Shazam!

752.   Shazbot!

753.   Sheep!

754.   Sheesh Kabobs!

755.   Sheesh!

756.   Shenanigans!

757.   Shhh and Holy Water!

758.   Shiatsu!

759.   Shiest!

760.   Shikaka!

761.   Shikamooney Catchatooey!

762.   Ship!

763.   Shish Kabob!

764.   Shitake Mushrooms on a Stick!

765.   Shitake Mushrooms!

766.   Shitickens!

767.   Shiznit!

768.   Shizz!

769.   Shizzle!

770.   Shmeesh!

771.   Shnit!

772.   Shnizz!

773.   Shnizzle!

774.   Shnoodles!

775.   Shnookerdookies!

776.   Shoobies!

777.   Shoot!

778.   Shoota Monkey!

779.   Shootdarn!

780.   Shoskovich!

781.   Shtuff!

782.   Shuckerdoodles!

783.   Shucks!

784.   Shuckydarn!

785.   Shut the Faucet Off!

786.   Shut the Front Door!

787.   Shut the Full Cup!

788.   Shut the Full Cup!

789.   Shut the Fup!

790.   Shut the Uck Fup!

791.   Shut Your Pie Hole!

792.   Shuzzbutt!

793.   Six and Two is Eight!

794.   Skittlefarts!

795.   Smack a Dog!

796.   Smeg Off!

797.   Smeg!

798.   Smeggin' Hell!

799.   Smeghead!

800.   SMH!

801.   Smurf It!

802.   Smurf This!

803.   Smurf!

804.   Snagglefraggle!

805.   Snails!

806.   Snap Crackle Pop!

807.   **Snap Dangity!**

808.   Snapdragon!

809.   Snapple Caps!

810.   Snarfblatt!

811.   Sneezing Hot Pockets!

812.   Snickerdoodle!

813.   Snicklefritz!

814.   Snit!

815.   Snot Buckets!

816.   Snot!

817.   Sod It!

818.   Son of a Bacon Bit!

819.   Son of a Baptist Preacher!

820.   Son of a Basket Weaver!

821. Son of a Batch of Cookies!

822. Son of a Batman!

823. Son of a Bee Sting!

824. Son of a Beehive!

825. Son of a Biscuit Eater!

826. Son of a Biscuit!

827. Son of a Bleep!

828. Son of a Booger Butt!

829. Son of a Brachiosaurus!

830. Son of a Buckenheimer!

831. Son of a Buckeroo!

832. Son of a Bucket!

833. Son of a Businessman!

834. Son of a Butt!

835. Son of a Cake Lover!

836. Son of a Cheeto!

837. Son of a Gun!

838. Son of a Monkey!

839.   Son of a Mother Trucker!

840.   Son of a Motherless Goat!

841.   Son of a Nutcracker!

842.   Son of a Pup!

843.   Son of a Puppet!

844.   Son of a Sea Cook!

845.   Son of a Sea Slug!

846.   Son of a Squeegee!

847.   Son of a Turkey Fart!

848.   Son of a Witch!

849.   Son of an Apple Pie!

850.   Son of Poseidon!

851.   Spiny Lumpsucker!

852.   Spit in My Biscuit!

853.   Splinters!

854.   Sprew You!

855.   Sprinkles!

856.   Squirrel!

857.   Sticky Wickett!

858.   Stomach Cramps!

859.   Stupid Head!

860.   Stupify!

861.   Suck Eggs!

862.   Suck It!

863.   Suck me Sideways!

864.   Sufferin' Succotash!

865.   Suffering Savior!

866.   Sugar Babies!

867.   Sugar Boogers!

868.   Sugar Honey iced Tea!

869.   Sugar Pastries!

870.   Sugar puffs!

871.   Sugar!

872.   Sugarfoot!

873.   Sugarplums!

874.   Sugartilt!

875.   Sunk in a Ditch!

876.   Supercalifragilisticexpialidocious!

877.   Surely You Jest!

878.   Swear Word!

879.   Swear!

880.   Sweet baby Hey Zeus!

881.   Sweet Gherkin!

882.   Sweet Home Alabama!

883.   Sweet Mamma Jamma!

884.   Sweet Merciful Crap!

885.   Sweet Niblets!

886.   Sweet Onions!

887.   Sweet Peas!

888.   Sweet Sassy Molassy

889.   Sweet Sugar!

890.   Sweet Zombie Jesus!

891.   Swizzle Sticks!

892.   Tabernacle!

893.   Take a Flying Leap!

894.   Take a Hike!

895.   Tarnation!

896.   Tartar Sauce!

897.   Teetering Teapots!

898.   Text You!

899.   That Just Burns My Biscuits!

900.   That's a Crock of Billy Baloney!

901.   That's a Load of Bunk!

902.   Thunder!

903.   Thunderation!

904.   Thundering Typhoon!

905.   Toots!

906.   Tosh!

907.   Tosser!

908.   Tottering Tadpoles!

909.   Trans Am it All!

910.   Trembling Tattooed Taiwanese Tyrants!

911.   Tripe!

912.   Troll Bogeys!

913.   Trouty Mouth!

914.   Truck Nuts!

915.   Truck!

916.   Tuck Fard!

917.   Turd!

918.   Turkey Buzzard!

919.   Tush!

920.   Twit!

921.   Uncle Ubb's Umbrella!

922.   Uranus!

923.   Urgh!

924.   Villification!

925.   Vlacas!

926.   Voldemort's Nipple!

927.   Vulgar Language!

928.   Vulgarity!

929.   Wanker!

930.   Wart Mouth!

931.   Well I'll be Shipped in Dip!

932.   Well, Doesn't That Bruise Your Banana?

933.   What a Load of Patootie!

934.   What a Pain!

935.   What in the Blue Blazes!

936.   What in the Name of Ron Weasley's Left

    Buttock!

937.   What in the Wide World of Sports?

938.   What the Bob Barker!

939.   What the Buck?

940.   What the Cat Hair?

941.   What the Cluck?

942.   What the Crab Cakes?

943.   What the Cuss!

944.   What the Devil?

945.   What the Eff!

946.   What the Fa-La-La?

947.   What the Fig Newtons!

948.   What the Flabberghast?

949.   What the Flagnog?

950.   What the Flutecake?

951.   What the French Toast?

952.   What the Frick Frack?

953.   What the Fridge!

954.   What the Frog!

955.   What the Fuzzy No-No?

956.   What the Gummy!

957.   What the Halo!

958.   What the Hello Kitty?

959.   What the Hey!

960.   What the Junk?

961.   What the Kronkie?

962.   What the Meow!

963.   What the Smurf?

964.   What the Snail?

965.   What the What?

966.   Whisker Biscuit!

967.   Whoa, Mama!

968.   Whoopsie Doodles!

969.   Whoopsie!

970.   Why You Little!

971.   Wicked Witch!

972.   William Shatner!

973.   Wingardium Leviosa!

974.   Wingnut!

975.   Witch!

976.   Witch's Warts!

977.   Wizz Off!

978.   Woe is Me!

979.   Wolfgang Amadeus Mozart!

980.   Woopsy Daisy!

981.   Wowie Zowie!

982.   Wowsers!

983.   WTF!

984.   Wyatt Earp!

985.   Yargh!

986.   Yee Haw!

987.   Yikes!

988.   Yippie Ki-Yay!

989.   Yo Mama!

990.   You Clock Clicker!

991.   You Cusshead!

992.   You Iceholes!

993.   Your God!

994.   Your Goodness!

995.   Yowza!

996.   Yuck fou!

997.   Zippity Doo Da!

998.   Zoinks!

999.   Zooks!

1000.   Zounds!

1001.   Zuzu's Petals!

About the Author

T. Cathers-Mitchell is a writer and amateur artist. She has published several successful articles online, both personally and professionally. She currently authors a personal blog, sharing her journey to recovery from PTSD through her writing and artwork. You can visit her blog at http://tcathersmitchell.blogspot.com. She currently lives in Door County, Wisconsin with her wife and two autistic children.

12429049R00036

Printed in Great Britain
by Amazon